WITHDRAWN

SELECTED POEMS

Marina Tsvetayeva

Tsvetaeva

SELECTED POEMS

Translated by
Elaine Feinstein

with a Foreword by
Max Hayward

London

OXFORD UNIVERSITY PRESS

NEW YORK   TORONTO

1971

Oxford University Press, Ely House, London W. 1

GLASGOW NEW YORK TORONTO MELBOURNE WELLINGTON
CAPE TOWN SALISBURY IBADAN NAIROBI DAR ES SALAAM LUSAKA ADDIS ABABA
BOMBAY CALCUTTA MADRAS KARACHI LAHORE DACCA
KUALA LUMPUR SINGAPORE HONG KONG TOKYO

ISBN 0 19 211803 X

*Printed in Great Britain by
Richard Clay (The Chaucer Press), Ltd.,
Bungay, Suffolk*

CONTENTS

FOREWORD

What shall I do . . .
with all this immensity in a measured world?

The best way to define Marina Tsevtayeva's place in modern
Russian poetry is to say that she had none—this was her personal
tragedy and her lonely distinction as an artist. There is a Russian
expression about a person who is frantically at odds with himself
and the life around him: 'he cannot find a place for himself'. The
phrase comes to mind as one reads the bare facts of Tsvetayeva's
biography. On her mother's side she was of cultivated Polish–
German descent—a heredity which, like Alexander Blok's, could
account for her fatefully romantic strain—and of the humblest
Russian rural origins on her father's. 'Common labourer and lady
of leisure' was how she summed up her family background in
a poem: it does much to explain the unique combination of
strength and refinement in her verse, the writing of which, she
always insisted, was a trade or a craft. She grew up in pre-
Revolutionary Moscow and was exposed to all the swirling cross-
currents of the so-called 'Silver Age' of Russian literature. Though
she herself remained aloof from all the various movements—
Symbolism, Futurism, Acmcism—she was formed by the same
climate as her almost exact contemporaries and peers, Pasternak,
Akhmatova, Gumilev, Mandelstam, and Mayakovsky, and she
was only twelve years younger than Blok, the presiding genius of
this extraordinary rebirth of Russian poetry (some of the poems
in the present volume are dedicated to him). As a young woman
she thus lived in the world so well evoked in the early chapters of
Dr. Zhivago, and it may not be fanciful to believe that there is
something of her in Lara who likewise could never 'find her place'
and was meant by Pasternak to symbolize Russia's torments in the

revolutionary decades: how much he identified Tsvetayeva with the epoch is shown by his several poetic tributes to her.

Her first volume of poetry appeared in 1910, when she was only sixteen, and was noticed and praised by Gumilev and others—they were impressed by the stark, down-to-earth quality, the 'common-labourer' side of her which always appealingly corrects her romantic tendencies—a very Russian trait.

In 1912, she married a publisher, Sergei Efron, a future White Officer and later, in emigration, Soviet sympathizer whose role in her life was tragically similar to that of the two men, Komarovsky and Zhivago, in Lara's.

At the beginning of the First World War, typically against the current, she flaunted her German roots in lines where she talked of 'Germany my madness, Germany my love'. The main significance of this was that, as always during her life, she was stubbornly, self-destructively determined to be 'quite contrary'. During the Revolution and Civil War she marked herself off from most of her fellow-poets and intellectuals—and later condemned herself to physical separation from them—by opting for the White cause. Whatever reservations they may have had about the Bolsheviks, few went as far as she in active commitment to the Volunteer Army. But, as her sister says in a recently published memoir, she was always drawn to anything doomed.

Her romantic illusions about a White Vendée painfully drained away in the squalor of emigré existence, in the suburbs first of Prague and then (from 1926) of Paris. The misery of all this, as well as her haughty isolation from all possible worlds, is well conveyed in 'Homesickness' (1934, p. 44, of the present volume). Yet much of her finest work was written in these years: 'Poem of the Mountain' and 'Poem of the End'—two lyrical sequels to characteristically impossible loves—and her epic adaptation of the German story of the Pied Piper and other long poems based on Russian folklore, as well as her verse dramas on classical themes ('Theseus', 'Phaedra' and 'Ariadne'), and many cycles of shorter poems, of which those on Czechoslovakia translated here are outstanding examples.

Despite Tsvetayeva's explicit hostility to the Soviet system, her independence of spirit, her identification by some emigré critics with Pasternak and others who were felt to have compromised themselves by staying in the Soviet Union, and, most of all, her husband's involvement in the early thirties with Soviet activities abroad, led to her gradual estrangement from the emigration. In 1937, after allegedly playing some part in the assassination of the defected Soviet agent, Ignacy Reiss, Efron disappeared from Paris and returned to the Soviet Union. Their daughter, Ariadne Efron, had gone back a little earlier, at the beginning of the same year. Two years later, in 1939, Marina followed them with her fourteen-year-old son, Georgi. The events that followed were sickeningly inevitable. Like so many loyal Soviet agents returning from abroad at the time of the Great Terror, Efron was arrested and executed for his pains—unknown to Marina, he had already been killed by the time she arrived in Moscow to join him. After eking out some kind of living as a translator for a couple of years, she was sent in 1941 to the small town of Yelabuga in the Tartar 'Autonomous Republic'. Her daughter and sister (who had never left Russia) had been sent to concentration camps, from which they emerged only years later (both are still alive in Moscow). After vain appeals for help to a prominent fellow poet, Marina hanged herself on 31 August 1941. There are no reliable accounts of what led to this final despair—anxiety for her son, who was later killed in the war, played a part—but, now aged forty-eight, she had clearly lived at the outer rim of the humanly bearable for too long.

In a sense, these scant external facts are less important for an understanding of her than the temperament which made some-thing like them necessary. Poets, more than other people, shape their own lives, and she would have found tragedy even if she had not lived at a time and in circumstances where tragedy so readily found her. The same was true, in even more striking fashion, of Osip Mandelstam, to whom she felt particularly close (but not of Pasternak, because such extremities were just not in his nature!).

However, if one tries to define her fate and her art in terms of her affinities to others, it is Vladimir Mayakovsky who, paradoxically, first comes to mind. Their closeness was not lost on Tsvetayeva herself who once referred to him, in a punning Russian phrase, as her 'dear enemy' (*rodnoi vrag*), and on his suicide in 1930, far from joining some of the emigrés in expressions of contempt and hatred for his memory, she wrote a cycle of seven poems in his honour (this, too, contributed to her parting of the ways with the emigration). It is only a seeming paradox that the self-appointed troubadour of the Revolution should have been so akin to one who devoted her poetic gift, with equal passion, to the cause of the Revolution's mortal enemies: her cycle entitled *Swans' camp*, written between 1917 and 1921, but published in full only long after her death, is perhaps the finest poetry to which the White movement can legitimately lay claim. The bond between her and Mayakovsky was, of course, in the astonishing similarity of their poetic and human temperaments, which forced both of them to seek in public causes the abnegation of self demanded by their unfulfillable natures; that they did so in opposite political camps was fortuitous. In both cases this search led them into a dead-end and then inexorably to suicide. It is not surprising, therefore, that the *accent* of their verse is so much alike in its general effect, even if not in its actual devices. Hammering, as it were, against the outer limits of their own being, they did what one can only call violence to the language, twisting and wrenching and pounding it, as a sculptor might wrestle with some tough, barely pliant material. This artistically controlled violence to language was their therapy and it gave rise to a peculiar, taut energy in their verse which Elaine Feinstein has providentially captured in her renderings of Tsvetayeva. This could only be achieved by careful attention to the peculiar techniques—unique in Russian prosody—which underlie the urgent, almost panting rhythm of Tsvetayeva's lines—she can always be recognized by the thud, like a heartbeat, of her monosyllabic masculine rhymes (more Anglo-Saxon than Russian in quality), and pauses in odd places.

But there was a great difference between Tsvetayeva and Mayakovsky. Whatever they may have had in common by way of their *goût de l'absolu*, vulnerability and treatment of language, she nevertheless belonged to a more select company. This was not only by virtue of her incomparably greater culture and taste, but also because she possessed a moral power which Mayakovsky either never had or dissipated in hollow public posturings. Marina Tsvetayeva's unflinching integrity in the employment of her genius puts her among the small band of Russian poet-witnesses who felt themselves to be, and recognized in each other the voices of the country and the keepers of its values during what Blok called the 'terrible years'. There were only four of them—besides Tsvetayeva: Pasternak, Akhmatova and Mandelstam. The last of them to die was Akhmatova who, towards the end of her life, in 1961, wrote about them all in a remarkable poem entitled quite simply: 'There are four of us'. By numbering Marina Tsvetayeva—the only one mentioned by name—among this chosen few, Akhmatova at last gave her the place she was never able to find in her life.

TRANSLATOR'S INTRODUCTION

. . . while the rest of us were still so tongue-tied that we could only be original despite ourselves . . . Aseyev and Tsvetayeva spoke like human beings. . . . Tsvetayeva's early manner . . . was exactly what all the symbolists, from first to last, dreamed of and did not achieve. And while they spluttered helplessly in their linguistic ocean of lifeless schemes and dead archaic forms, Tsvetayeva soared over the real difficulties of creation, solving its problems effortlessly and with matchless technical skill. . . . It was not until the spring of 1922, after she had left Russia, that I came across a volume of her *versty* in a Moscow bookshop. I was immediately overcome by the immense lyrical power of her poetic form. It was a form which had sprung living from experience—personal, and neither narrow-chested nor short of breath from line to line but rich and compact and enveloping sequences of stanza after stanza in its vast periods of unbroken rhythm.

Boris Pasternak, *Essay in Autobiography* (1957)

It was this passage, read some years ago, which first sent me to find the poetry of Marina Tsvetayeva. I wanted, simply, to read her; perhaps to learn from her. And the first surprise was that her poems still existed only in Russian. What she had written in 1933, in exile and neglect, remained close to the truth. 'I went abroad in 1922, and my reader remained in Russia where my poems no longer penetrate. . . . And thus, I am here without readers; in Russia, without books.'

In the sixties, however, twenty years after her death, a Soviet edition of her poems *had* appeared.[1] I was able to go to this with the help of Angela Livingstone of the Department of Literature,

[1] Marina Tsvetayeva: *Izbrannye proizvedeniya* (Moscow–Leningrad, 1965). There was also a volume of her poems published in Munich: *Lebediny stan. Stikhi, 1917–1921*, ed. by Gleb Struve (1957).

University of Essex, who provided me with annotated word-for-word translations. Without her detailed and generous collaboration, this book could not have gone forward. I began to work through some of the lyrics from 'The Poem of the End'; a sequence of poems no one can read coldly. Very soon I became obsessed with the sense that there was nothing like Tsvetayeva in English. It was not only the violence of her emotions, or the ferocity of her expression. I was overcome with admiration for the extraordinary wholeness of her self-exposure.

By this time I had learnt enough of her life to be astonished at the personal stamina which must have sustained that achievement. Her whole life was a history of loss.[1] She watched the devastation of her country by a revolution she did not support. In the Moscow famine one of her children died in a state orphanage. In 1922 she left Russia to follow her husband Sergei Efron, and in a long exile she saw her early fame vanish, and learnt to accept growing loneliness and rejection. Her marriage and her many passionate love-affairs were largely ill-fated; her most intense experience of love seems to have occurred during the few years she lived in Prague; and she records the ending of that in 'The Poem of the Mountain' and 'The Poem of the End'. The one central and continuing reality of her life was poetry and her loyalty to individual poets which ran across the political boundaries of the time. So it is not surprising that she did not long hold the enthusiasm of the distinguished group of Russian émigrés who lived in Paris. As a poet she felt her exile bitterly. Yet when she returned to Russia in 1939, following Efron who had been exposed as a Soviet agent, she found herself completely without friends and without work. Efron was very probably shot. When war came she was evacuated to Yelabuga, and there in 1941 she hanged herself. And yet Marina Tsvetayeva was a woman who had 'always loved life so much', as her friend Anna Tesková wrote when the news of her death reached her.

Inevitably there are gaps in our present knowledge of that life,

[1] See Simon Karlinsky, *Marina Cvetaeva—Her Life and Art* (Berkeley and Los Angeles, 1966).

especially in relation to her husband and children. She felt isolated, always; and it seems clear enough that she did not choose the form of her isolation. She seems always to have needed the love of friends and the company of poets. And yet there is something inevitable in the way she antagonized, for instance, the Russian émigrés in Paris who had initially welcomed her with honour. As she said in a letter to Ivask in 1933: 'In the emigration they at first (hotheadedly) publish me, then having come to their senses, withdraw me from circulation, having realized that there is something in me that is not theirs: it is from over there.'

The émigrés were not mistaken; Tsvetayeva's allegiance to the poets 'over there'—in Soviet Russia—was continuous. In 1926, when Efron with two others began the magazine *Versty*, it included Pasternak, Babel, and Yesenin, along with Tsvetayeva. And when the news of Mayakovsky's suicide reached the West, Tsvetayeva refused to sign the notorious émigré letter which read in part: '*Quelles que puissent être les nuances possibles quant à l'appréciation du talent poétique de Maiakovsky, nous, les écrivains russes, mieux informés que les étrangers de la situation actuelle de notre littérature, nous affirmons que Maiakovsky n'a jamais été un grand poète russe. . . .*' Later she defended Yesenin and Mayakovsky as poets, against the powerful figure of Bunin, in *Poet o Kritike*, which must have sealed her unpopularity. No wonder she felt as she wrote in a letter to Anna Tesková: 'In Paris, with rare personal exceptions, everyone hates me, they write all sorts of nasty things, leave me out in all sorts of ways, and so on.'[1]

Her happiest time, she came to feel, in spite of her tragic love-affair, had been spent in Prague. There a whole city had been suffused for her with a sense of intense, if painful, vitality. In 1926, she is already writing to Anna Tesková of her desire to return there. 'In that same Chekhia one can live humanly; I have lived inhumanly and I'm tired of living like that, I'm tired in advance.' She wanted to find some place in the centre of the city where it would be possible for her to visit galleries and attend

[1] Letter no. 31, Meudon, Easter 1927. Marina Tsvetayeva, *Pis'ma k Anne Teskovoi* (*Letters to Anna Tesková*) (Academia Praha, Prague 1969).

concerts, and enjoy the city's richness, without being wholly bound to her house by the need to look after her children.

She must have been an eccentric, impractical, and probably an over-demanding person; many speak of the antagonism she roused in them, though it is clear that she also aroused enduring friendships. Osip Mandelstam, to whom she offers Moscow in a sequence of poems in 1916, was clearly in love with her, and dedicated a number of his poems to her. But many of her most intense and valued relationships were sustained, at a distance, through letters. Pasternak, for instance, can have met her seldom after 1918; and yet he was willing to write to Gorky on her behalf; and on her side, she offered a homage approaching awe to the barely known figure of Alexander Blok, who embodied for her what she felt to be the essentially supernatural quality of poetry itself.

Tsvetayeva spoke of poetry as Emily Dickinson did in the famous letter to a bewildered Higginson: 'If I read a book and it makes my whole body so cold I know no fire can ever warm me, I know that is poetry. If I feel physically as if the top of my head were taken off, I know that is poetry. These are the only ways I know it. Is there any other way?'

There were many other ways current in Tsvetayeva's time; and most of them were concerned, one way or another, with putting poetry to the service of social good. For Tsvetayeva essentially the true poet could never do anything so willed, since she was the victim of a kind of visitation. In 'Art in the Light of Conscience' she declared: 'Blok wrote *The Twelve* in a single night, and got up in complete exhaustion, like one who has been driven upon.'[1] For 'the condition of creation' was for her analogous to dreaming, when suddenly 'obeying an unknown necessity, you set fire to a house or push your friend down from the mountain top'. The least egotistical of poets, though so many of her greatest poems arose from her own pain, she preserved what to her was the essential demand of poetry: 'To let the ear hear, the hand race (and when it doesn't race—to stop),' and you can

[1] All quotations from 'Art in the Light of Conscience' are taken from the translation by Angela Livingstone and Valentina Coe.

sense that abandonment of self in the very movement of her lines, in their onward, compelled, flow.

Tsvetayeva was a sincere admirer of Akhmatova, to whom she wrote several poems, and inevitably their names occur together in any account of the poetry of the period. But they are very different creatures. And the difference is perhaps best defined by Blok himself, in a remark Tsvetayeva refers to in her essay 'Art in the Light of Conscience' as that cruel thing Blok said about the early Akhmatova, that she 'wrote verse as if a man were looking at her, but you should write it as if God is looking at you'.

This could be misleading. For although, talking about Rilke, Tsvetayeva speaks of poems as *prayer*, she did not make the mistake of blurring the distinction between poetry and religion, any more that she would ever allow for poetry the utilitarian hope that Art can do civic good. Both were as much *limitations* she recognized in poetry, as magniloquent claims made for it. In the closing passage from 'Art in the Light of Conscience' she makes that clear: 'To be a human being is more important, because it is more needed. . . . The doctor and the priest are humanly more important, all the others are socially more important.'

It is always a false polarity to set life in opposition to art except in this way; to see the limitations of the claim that can be made for it. Certainly it is in what Tsvetayeva's poetry *includes* that we sense its greatness; there is no censor between her and her experience, nothing that checks what is given to her from finding its shape upon the page. And yet she understood very well the ambiguous relation she took up to the external world. 'I don't love life as such; for me it begins to signify, that is to acquire weight and meaning only when it is transformed, that is—in art. If I were to be taken beyond the ocean, into Paradise, and for-bidden to write, I would refuse the ocean and Paradise.'

There is nothing wilful in this; it is simply the other side of the truth she records sadly and honestly, in another letter. 'Externally, things always go badly with me, because I don't love it (the external), I take no account of it, I don't give it the required importance and demand *nothing* from it. Everything

B   xvii

that I love changes from an external thing into an inward one, from the moment of my love of it it stops being external.' She takes no pride in this, though as she makes clear at the conclusion of 'Art in the Light of Conscience' she 'would not exchange her work for any other. Aware of greater things, I do lesser ones, this is why there is no forgiveness for me. Only such as I will be held responsible at the Judgement of Conscience. But if there is a Judgement Day of the word, at that I am guiltless.'

It was with a sense of some temerity, as well as enormous excitement, that I began to try and find an English poetic equivalent for her eccentric Russian genius. All translation is difficult; Tsvetayeva is a particularly difficult poet. No line by line version could catch her passionate, onward flow. And her pauses and sudden changes of speed were felt always against the deliberate constraint of the forms she had chosen. Perhaps the exact metres could not be kept, but some sense of her shapeliness, as well as her roughness, had to survive.

For this reason I have invariably followed her stanzaic patterning, though I have frequently indented lines where she does not. This slight shift is one of many designed to dispel any sense of static solidity, which blocks of lines convey to an English eye, and which is not induced by the Russian.

There were other structural changes. It was impossible to preserve all her startling distortions of word order, in an uninflected language like English, without dangerously confusing the reader. Some repetitions had to be sacrificed to preserve the pattern of her rhythms. The very compactness of Russian and its polysyllabic structure were severe problems, the more harrowing because she makes such brilliant use of them. Sometimes, so that a poem could move forward in a natural English syntax, connective words had to be introduced, and in the process, and against my will, I observed that some of her abruptness had been smoothed out, and the poem had gained a different, more logical scheme of development. There were other problems. Tsvetayeva's punctuation is strongly individual; but to have reproduced it pedantically would often have destroyed the tone of the English version. A gap usually seemed closer to the movement of her line than a dash and, although I retained her dashes where they indicated the beginning of direct speech, I preferred otherwise to keep only those that seemed irreplaceable. I also frequently left out exclamation marks where their presence seemed to weaken a line that was already loud and vibrant. Furthermore, there were difficulties of diction. Words with echoes of ancient folk-song and the Bible, of which there are many, were particularly hard to carry across into English.

I am not sure, as I think of these problems, how far a discussion of methods of translation attracts much useful reflection, or how far it can bear on what Octavio Paz calls the 'transformation' of a poem from one language to another. Poems are not translated *consistently*. Every line proposes a new set of possibilities. And with a poet such as Tsvetayeva, whose movement extends through many stanzas, the process was often a matter of reading towards every problematic line again and again from the opening of the English version, to be sure the total movement had been sustained. Nor do I understand why occasionally a translator will suddenly have the sense of writing the poem itself, freshly, as though for the first time, while on other occasions every painstaking draft appears to die under the hand. Most often, I suppose, Angela Livingstone and I shared a sense of compromise. Or, if the transformation altogether refused to happen, regretfully, we left the poem out of our selection.

I should like to acknowledge further debts of gratitude: to Valentina Coe, who helped with some of the more intractable Russian poems; and made a literal version of 'The Poem of the Mountain'; to Leslie Milne and Dr. Nikolai Andreyev. I should also like to thank the editors of the *London Magazine* and *Modern Poetry in Translation*, who published certain of these poems; and the Arts Council of Great Britain, without whose grant this work would have taken even longer to complete

I know the truth—give up all other truths!
No need for people anywhere on earth to struggle.
Look—it is evening, look, it is nearly night:
what do you speak of, poets, lovers, generals?

The wind is level now, the earth is wet with dew,
the storm of stars in the sky will turn to quiet.
And soon all of us will sleep under the earth, we
who never let each other sleep above it.

1915

What is this gypsy passion for separation, this
    readiness to rush off   when we've just met?
My head rests in my hands as I
    realize, looking into the night

that no one turning over our letters has
    yet understood how completely and
how deeply faithless we are, which is
    to say: how true we are to ourselves.

1915

We shall not escape Hell, my passionate
sisters, we shall drink black resins—
we who sang our praises to the Lord
with every one of our sinews, even the finest,

we did not lean over cradles or
spinning wheels at night, and now we are
carried off by an unsteady boat
under the skirts of a sleeveless cloak,

we dressed every morning in
fine Chinese silk, and we would
sing our paradisal songs at
the fire of the robbers' camp,

slovenly needlewomen, (all
our sewing came apart), dancers,
players upon pipes: we have been
the queens   of the whole world!

first scarcely covered by rags,
then with constellations in our hair, in
gaol and at feasts we have
bartered away heaven,

in starry nights, in the apple
orchards of Paradise.
—Gentle girls, my beloved sisters,
we shall certainly find ourselves in Hell!

1915

3

We are keeping an eye on the girls, so that the *kvass*
doesn't go sour in the jug, or the pancakes cold,
counting over the rings, and pouring Anis
into the long bottles with their narrow throats,

straightening tow thread for the peasant woman:
filling the house with the fresh smoke of
incense   and we are sailing over Cathedral square
arm in arm with our godfather, silks thundering.

The wet nurse has a screeching cockerel
in her apron—her clothes are like the night.
She announces in an ancient whisper that
a dead young man   lies in the chapel.

And an incense cloud wraps the corners
under its own saddened chasuble.
The apple trees are white, like angels—and
the pigeons on them—grey—like incense itself.

And the pilgrim woman sipping *kvass* from the ladle
on the edge of the couch, is telling
to the very end a tale about Razin
and his most beautiful Persian girl.

1916

No one has taken anything away—
    there is even a sweetness for me in being apart.
I kiss you now across the many
    hundreds of miles that separate us.

I know: our gifts are unequal, which is
    why my voice is   quiet, for the first time.
What can my untutored verse
    matter to you, a young Derzhavin?

For your terrible flight I give you blessing.
    Fly, then, young eagle! You
have stared into the sun without blinking.
    Can my young gaze be too heavy for you?

No one has ever stared more
    tenderly or more fixedly after you . . .
I kiss you   across hundreds of
    separating years.

                    1916

You throw back your head, because
you are proud. And a braggart.
This February has
brought me a gay companion!

Clattering with gold pieces, and
slowly puffing out smoke, we
walk like solemn foreigners
throughout my native city.

And whose attentive hands have
touched your eyelashes, beautiful boy, and
when or how many times your
lips have been kissed

I do not ask. That dream my thirsty
spirit has conquered. Now
I can honour in you the
divine boy, ten years old!

Let us wait by the river that
rinses the coloured beads of street-lights:
I shall take you as far as the square
that has witnessed adolescent Tsars.

Whistle out your boyish
pain, your heart squeezed in your hand.
My indifferent and crazy creature—
now set free—goodbye!

1916

Where does this tenderness come from?
These are not the   first curls I
have stroked slowly   and lips I
have known are   darker than yours

as stars rise often and go out again
(where does this tenderness come from?)
so many eyes have risen and died out
    in front of these eyes of mine.

and yet no such song have
I heard in the darkness of night before,
(where does this tenderness come from?):
    here, on the ribs of the singer.

Where does this tenderness come from?
And what shall I do with it, young
sly singer, just passing by?
Your lashes are   longer than anyone's.

                              1916

Bent with worry, God
    paused, to smile.
And look, there were many
holy angels with bodies of

the radiance he had
    given them,
some with enormous wings and
others without any,

which is why I weep
    so much
because even more than God
himself I love his fair angels.

                    1916

Today or tomorrow the snow will melt.
You lie alone beneath an enormous fur.
Shall I pity you? Your lips
have gone dry for ever.

Your drinking is difficult, your step heavy.
Every passer-by hurries away from you.
Was it with fingers like yours that Rogozhin
clutched the garden knife?

And the eyes, the eyes in your face!
Two circles of charcoal, year-old circles!
Surely when you were still young your girl
lured you into a joyless house.

Far away—in the night—over asphalt—a cane.
Doors—swing open into—night—under beating wind.
Come in! Appear! Undesired guest! Into
my chamber which is—most bright!

1916

Verses about Moscow

I

There are clouds   about us
and domes   about us:
over the whole of Moscow
so many hands are needed!
I lift you up like a
sapling, my best burden: for
to me you are   weightless.

In this city of wonder
this peaceful city
I shall be joyful, even
when I am dead. You
shall reign, or grieve
or perhaps receive my crown:
for you are my first born!

When you fast   in Lent
do not blacken your brows
and honour the churches—these
forty times forty   go
about on foot   stride youthfully
over the whole seven of
these untrammelled hills.

Your turn will come.
You will give Moscow
with tender bitterness
to your daughter also

As for me   unbroken sleep
and the sound of bells
in the surly dawn of
the *Vagankovo* cemetery.

Strange and beautiful brother   take this
city no hands built   out of my hands!

Church by church   all the forty times forty, and
the small pigeons also that rise over them.

Take the Spassky gate, with its flowers, where
the orthodox remove their caps, and

the chapel of stars, that refuge from evil,
where the floor is   polished by kisses.

Take from me the incomparable circle
of five cathedrals, ancient, holy friend!

I shall lead you as a guest from another
country to the Chapel of the Inadvertent Joy

where pure gold domes will begin to shine
for you, and sleepless bells will start thundering.

There the Mother of God will drop her
cloak upon you from the crimson clouds

and you will rise up filled with wonderful powers.
Then, you will not repent that you have loved me!

5

Over the city that great Peter rejected
rolls out the thunder of the bells.

A thundering surf has overturned upon
this woman you have now rejected.

I offer homage to Peter and you also,
yet above you both the bells remain

and while they thunder from that blueness, the
primacy of Moscow cannot be questioned

for all the forty times forty churches
laugh above the arrogance of Tzars.

7

There are seven hills   like seven bells,
seven bells, seven bell-towers. Every
one of the forty times forty churches, and the
seven hills of bells have been numbered.

On a day of bells I was born, it was
the golden day of John the Divine.
The house was gingerbread surrounded by
wattle-fence, and small churches with gold heads.

And I loved it, I loved the first ringing,
the nuns flowing towards Mass, and
the wailing in the stone, the heat of sleeping—
the sense of a soothsayer in the neighbouring house.

Come with me, people of Moscow, all of you,
Imbecile, thieving, flagellant mob!
And priest: stop my mouth up firmly
with Moscow   which is a land of bells!

8

Moscow, what a vast
hostelry is your house!
Everyone in Russia is   homeless,
we shall all make our way towards you.

With shameful brands on our backs and
knives   stuck in the tops of our boots,
for you call us in to you
however far away we are,

because for the brand of the criminal
and for every known sickness
we have our healer here,
the Child Panteleimon.

Behind a small door where
people pour in their crowds
lies the Iversky heart—
red-gold and radiant

and a Hallelujah floods
over the burnished fields.
Moscow soil, I bend to
kiss your breast.

From Insomnia

2

As I love to
  kiss hands, and
to name everything, I
  love to open
doors!
  Wide   into the night!

Pressing my head
  as I listen to some
heavy step grow softer
  or the wind shaking
the sleepy and sleepless
  woods.

Ah, night
  small rivers of water rise
and bend towards   sleep.
  (I am nearly sleeping.)
Somewhere in the night a
  human being is drowning.

3

In my enormous city it is   night,
as from my sleeping house I go   out,
and people think perhaps I'm a daughter or wife
but in my mind is one thought only   night.

The July wind now sweeps a way for   me.
From somewhere, some window, music though   faint.
The wind can blow until the dawn   today,
in through the fine walls of the breast rib-cage.

Black poplars, windows, filled with   light.
Music from high buildings, in my hand a flower.
Look at my steps   following   nobody
Look at my shadow, nothing's here of me.

The lights   are like threads of golden beads
in my mouth is the taste of the night   leaf.
Liberate me from the bonds of   day,
my friends, understand: I'm nothing but your dream.

5

Now as a guest from heaven, I
    visit your country:
I have seen the vigil of the forests
    and sleep in the fields.

Somewhere in the night horseshoes
    have torn up the grass, and
there are cows breathing heavily in
    a sleepy cowshed.

Now let me tell you sadly and
    with tenderness of the
goose-watchman awake, and
    the sleeping geese,

of hands immersed in dog's wool,
    grey hair—a grey dog—
and how towards six
    the dawn is beginning.

6

Tonight—I am alone in the night,
    a homeless and sleepless nun!
Tonight I hold all the keys to this
    the only capital city

and lack of sleep guides me on my path.
    You are so lovely, my dusky Kremlin!
Tonight I put my lips to the breast
    of the whole round and warring earth.

Now I feel hair—like fur—standing on end:
    the stifling wind blows straight into my soul.
Tonight I feel compassion for everyone,
    those who are pitied, along with those who are kissed.

In the pine-tree, tenderly tenderly,
  finely finely: something hissed.
It is a child with black
  eyes that I see in my sleep.

From the fair pine-trees hot
  resin drips, and in this
splendid night there are
  saw-teeth going over my heart.

Black as   the centre of an eye, the centre, a blackness
that sucks at light. I love your vigilance

Night, first mother of songs, give me the voice to sing of you
in those fingers lies the bridle of the four winds.

Crying out, offering words of homage to you, I am
only a shell where the ocean is still sounding.

But I have looked too long into human eyes.
Reduce me now to ashes   Night, like a black sun.

Who sleeps at night? No one is sleeping.
   In the cradle a child is screaming.
An old man sits over his death, and anyone
   young enough talks to his love, breathes
into her lips, looks into her eyes.

Once asleep   who knows if we'll wake again?
We have time, we have time, we have time to sleep!

From house to house the sharp-eyed
   watchman goes with his pink lantern
and over the pillow scatters the rattle
   of his loud clapper, rumbling.

Don't sleep! Be firm! Listen, the alternative
is   everlasting sleep. Your   everlasting house!

Here's another window
with more sleepless people!
Perhaps   drinking wine or
perhaps only sitting,
or maybe two lovers are
unable to part hands.
Every house has
a window like this.

A window at night: cries
of meeting or leaving.
Perhaps   there are many lights,
perhaps   only three candles.
But there is no peace in
my mind anywhere, for
in my house also, these
things are beginning:

Pray for the wakeful house,
friend, and the lit window.

Poems for Akhmatova

Muse of lament, you are the most beautiful of
   all muses, a crazy emanation of white night:
and you have sent a black snow storm over all Russia.
   We are pierced with the arrows of your cries

so that we shy like horses at the muffled
   many times uttered pledge—Ah!—Anna
Akhmatova—the name is a vast sigh
   and it falls into depths without name

and we wear crowns only through stamping
   the same earth as you, with the same sky over us.
Whoever shares the pain of your deathly power will
   lie down immortal   upon his death bed.

In my melodious town the domes are burning
   and the blind wanderer praises our shining Lord.
I give you my town of many bells,
   Akhmatova, and with the gift: my heart.

I stand   head in my hands   thinking how
    unimportant are the traps we set for one another
I hold my head in my hands   as I sing
    in this late hour, in the late dawn.

Ah how violent is this wave which has
    lifted me up on to its crest: I sing
of one   that is unique among us
    as the moon is   alone in the sky,

that has flown into my heart like a raven,
    has speared into the clouds
hook-nosed, with deathly anger: even
    your favour is   dangerous,

for you have spread out your night
    over the pure gold of my Kremlin itself
and have tightened my throat with the pleasure
    of singing   as if with a strap.

Yes, I am happy, the dawn never
    burnt with more purity, I am
happy to give everything to you
    and to go away   like a beggar.

for I was the first to give you—
    whose voice   deep darkness!   has
constricted the movement of my breathing—
    the name of the Tsarskoselsky Muse.

3

I am a convict. You won't fall behind.
You are my guard. Our fate is therefore one.
And in that emptiness that we both share
the same command to ride away is given.

And now my demeanour is calm.
And now   my eyes are without guile.
Won't you set me free, my guard, and
let me walk now, towards that pine-tree?

4

You block out everything, even the sun
  at its highest, hold all the stars in your hand!
If only through   some wide open door, I
  could blow like the wind to where you are,

and starting to stammer, suddenly blushing,
  could lower my eyes before you
and fall quiet, in tears, as
  a child sobs to receive forgiveness.

1916

Poems for Blok

Your name is a   bird in my hand
a piece of   ice on the tongue
one single movement of the lips.
Your name is: five signs,
a ball caught in flight, a
silver bell in the mouth

a stone, cast in a quiet pool
makes the splash of your name, and
the sound is in the clatter of
night hooves, loud as a thunderclap
or it speaks straight into my forehead,
shrill as the click of a cocked gun.

Your name   how impossible, it
is a kiss in the eyes on
motionless eyelashes, chill and sweet.
Your name is a kiss of snow
a gulp of icy spring water, blue
as a dove. About your name is: sleep.

Tender   spectre
blameless as a knight, who
has called you into
my adolescent life?

In blue dark, grey
and priestly, you
stand here, dressed in snow.

And it's not the wind
that drives me through the town now.
No, this is the third
night I felt the old enemy.

With light blue eyes his
magic has bound
me, that snowy singer:

swan of snow, under
my feet he spreads his feathers.
Hovering feathers,
slowly they dip in the snow.

Thus upon feathers
I go, towards the door
behind which is: death.

He sings to me
behind the blue windows.
He sings to me
as jewelled bells.

Long is the shout from
his swan's beak as
he calls.

Dear spectre of
mist I know this is dreaming,
so one favour now, do
for me, amen: of dispersing.
Amen, amen.

You are going   west of the sun now.
You will see there   evening light.
You are going   west of the sun and
snow will cover up your tracks.

Past my windows   passionless
you are going in quiet snow.
Saint of God, beautiful, you
are the quiet light of my soul

but I do not long for your spirit.
Your way is indestructible.
And your hand is pale from holy
kisses, no nail of mine.

By your name I shall not call you.
My hands shall not stretch after you
to your holy waxen face I shall
only bow   from afar

standing under the slow falling snow, I shall
fall to my knees   in the snow.
In your holy name I shall only
kiss that evening snow

where, with majestic pace you
go by in tomb–like quiet,
the light of quiet   holy glory
of it: Keeper of my soul.

At home in Moscow   where the domes are burning,
at home in Moscow   in the sound of bells,
where I live the tombs   in their rows are standing
and in them Tsaritsas   are asleep and Tsars.

And you don't know how   at dawn the Kremlin is
the easiest place to   breathe in the whole wide earth
and you don't know when   dawn reaches the Kremlin
I pray to you until   the next day comes

and I go with you   by your river Neva
even while beside   the Moscow river
I am standing here   with my head lowered
and the line of street lights   sticks fast together.

With my insomnia   I love you wholly.
With my insomnia   I listen for you,
just at the hour throughout   the Kremlin, men
who ring the bells   begin to waken.

Still my river   and your river
still my hand   and your hand
will never join, or not until
one dawn catches up another dawning.

6

Thinking him   human   they
decided to kill him, and
now he's dead. For ever.
—Weep. For the dead angel.

At the day's setting, he
sang the evening beauty.
Three waxen lights now
shudder superstitiously

and lines of light, hot
strings across the snow come from him.
Three waxen candles.
To the sun. The light-bearer.

O now look how
dark his eyelids are fallen,
O now look how
his wings are broken.

The black reciter reads.
The people idly stamp.
Dead lies the singer, and
celebrates resurrection.

And the gadflies gather about indifferent cart-horses,
the red calico of Kaluga puffs out in the wind,
it is a time of whistling quails and huge skies,
bells waving over waves of corn, and more
talk about Germans than anyone can bear.
Now yellow, yellow, beyond the blue trees is a
cross, and a sweet fever, a radiance over
everything: your name   sounding like *angel*.

A weak shaft of light through the blackness of hell is
your voice under the rumble of exploding shells

in that thunder like a seraph he is announcing
in a toneless voice, from somewhere else, some

ancient misty morning he inhabits, how he
loved us, who are blind and nameless   who

share the blue cloak of   sinful treachery
and more tenderly than anyone loved the woman who

sank more daringly than any into the night   of evil,
and of his love for you, Russia, which he cannot end.

And he draws an absent-minded finger along
his temple   all the time he tells us of

the days that wait for us, how God will deceive us.
We shall call for the sun and it will not rise.

He spoke like a solitary prisoner
(or perhaps a child speaking to himself)

so that over the whole square the sacred
heart of Alexander Blok appeared to us.

Look there he is, weary from foreign parts,
a leader without body-guard.

There   he is drinking a mountain stream from his hands
a prince without native land.

He has everything in his holy princedom there
Army, bread and mother.

Lovely is your inheritance.
Govern, friend without friends.

1916–1927

A kiss on the head—wipes away misery.
I kiss your head.

A kiss on the eyes—takes away sleeplessness.
I kiss your eyes.

A kiss on the lips—quenches the deepest thirst.
I kiss your lips.

A kiss on the head—wipes away memory.
ı kiss your head.

Praise to the Rich

And so, making clear in advance
I know there are miles   between us;
and I reckon myself with the tramps, which
is a place of honour in this world:

under the wheels of luxury, at
table with cripples and hunchbacks. . . .
From the top of the bell-tower roof,
I proclaim it: I *love* the rich.

For their rotten, unsteady root
for the damage done in their cradle
for the absent-minded way their hands
go in and out of their pockets;

for the way their softest word is
obeyed like a shouted order; because
they will not be let into heaven; and
because they don't look in your eyes;

and because they send secrets   by courier!
and their passions   by errand boy.
In the nights that are thrust upon them they
kiss and drink   under compulsion,

and because in all their accountings
in boredom, in gilding, in wadding,
they can't buy me   I'm too brazen:
I confirm it, I *love* the rich!

and in spite of their shaven fatness,
their fine drink   (wink, and spend):
some   sudden   defeatedness
and a look that is like a dog's

doubting . . .
        the core of their balance
nought, but are the weights true?
I say that among all outcasts
there are no such orphans on earth.

There is also a nasty fable
about camels getting through needles
    for that look, surprised to death
apologizing for sickness, as

if they were suddenly bankrupt: 'I would have been
glad to lend, but' and their silence.
'I counted in carats once and then I was one of them.'
For all these things, I swear it: I *love* the rich.

1922

The Poet

A poet's speech begins   a great way off.
A poet is   carried far away by speech

by way of planets, signs, and the   ruts
of roundabout parables, between *yes* and *no*,
in his hands even sweeping gestures from a bell-tower
become hook-like. For the way of comets

is the poet's way. And the blown-apart
links of causality   are his links. Look up
after him without hope. The eclipses of
poets are not foretold in the calendar.

He is the one that mixes up the cards
and confuses   arithmetic and weight.
He is   the *questioner* from the desk
the one who beats Kant on the head,

the one in the stone graves of the Bastille
who remains like a tree in its loveliness.
And yet the one whose   traces have always vanished,
the train everyone always arrives
too late to catch

for the path of comets
is the path of poets: they burn without warming,
pick without cultivating. They are: an explosion, a breaking in—
and the mane of their path makes the   curve of a
graph   cannot be foretold by the calendar.

There are superfluous people about in
this world, out of sight, who
aren't listed in any directory: and
home for them is   a rubbish heap.

They are hollow, jostled creatures:
who keep silent, dumb as dung, they are
nails   catching in your silken hem
dirt   imagined under your wheels.

Here they are, ghostly and invisible, the
sign is on them, like the speck of the leper.
People like Job in this world who
might even have envied him. If.

We are poets, which has the sound of outcast.
Nevertheless, we step out from our shores.
We dare contend for godhead, with goddesses,
and for the Virgin   with the gods themselves.

3

Now what shall I do here, blind and fatherless?
Everyone else can see and has a father.
Passion in this world has to leap anathema
as it might be over the walls of a trench
and weeping   is called a cold in the head.

What shall I do, by nature and trade
a singing creature (like a wire—sunburn! Siberia!)
as I go over the bridge of my enchanted
visions, that cannot be weighed, in a
world that deals only in weights and measures?

What shall I do, singer and first-born, in a
world where the deepest black is grey,
and inspiration is kept in   a thermos?
with all this immensity
in a measured world?

An Attempt at Jealousy

How is your life with the other one,
   simpler, isn't it? One   stroke of the oar
then a long coastline, and soon
   even the memory of me

will be a floating island
   (in the sky, not on the waters):
spirits, spirits, you will be
   sisters, and never lovers.

How is your life with an ordinary
   woman? without godhead?
Now that your sovereign has
   been deposed (and you have stepped down).

How is your life? Are you fussing?
   flinching? How   do you get up?
The tax of deathless vulgarity
   can you cope with it, poor man?

—'Scenes and hysterics   I've had
   enough! I'll rent my own house.'
How is your life with the other one
   now, you that I chose for my own?

More to your taste, more delicious
   is it, your food? Don't moan if you sicken.
How is your life with an *image*
   you, who walked on Sinai?

How is your life with a stranger
    from this world? Can you (be frank)
love her? Or do you   feel shame
    like Zeus' reins on your forehead?

How is your life? Are you
    healthy? How do you   sing?
How do you deal with the pain
    of an undying conscience, poor man?

How is your life with a piece of market
    stuff, at a steep price.
After Carrara marble,
    how is your life with the dust of

plaster now? (God was hewn from
    stone, but he is smashed to bits.)
How do you live with one of a
    thousand women   after Lilith?

Sated with newness, are you?
    Now you are grown cold to magic,
how is your life with an
    earthly woman, without a sixth

sense? Tell me: are you happy?
    Not? In a shallow pit? How is
your life, my love? Is it as
    hard as mine with another man?

                        1924

                        43

Homesickness! that long
exposed weariness!
It's all the same to me now
where I am   altogether lonely

or what stones I wander over
home with a shopping bag to
a house that is no more mine
than a hospital or a barracks

It's all the same to me, captive
lion   what faces I move through
bristling, or what human crowd will
cast me out   as it must

into myself, into my separate internal
world, a Kamchatka bear without ice.
Where I fail to fit in (and I'm not trying) or
where I'm humiliated   it's all the same.

And I won't be seduced by the thought of
my native language, its milky call.
How can it matter   in what tongue I
am misunderstood by whoever I meet

(or by what readers, swallowing
newsprint, squeezing for gossip?)
They all belong to the twentieth
century, and   I am before time,

stunned, like a log left
behind from an avenue of trees.
People are all the same to me, everything
is the same, and it may be the most

indifferent of all   are these
signs and tokens which once were
native   but the dates have been
rubbed out: the soul was born somewhere.

For my country has taken so little care
of me that even the sharpest spy could
go over my whole spirit and would
detect no native stain there.

Houses are alien, churches are empty
everything   is the same:
But if by the side of the path one
particular bush rises
                         the rowanberry . . .

                                        1934

Readers of Newspapers

It crawls, the underground snake,
crawls, with its load of people.
And each one   has his
newspaper, his skin
disease; a twitch of chewing;
newspaper *caries*.
Masticators of gum,
readers of newspapers.

And who are the readers? old men? athletes?
soldiers? No face, no features,
no age. Skeletons—there's no
face, only the newspaper page.

All Paris   is dressed
this way from forehead to navel.
Give it up, girl, or
you'll give birth to
a reader of newspapers.

Sway/ he lived with his sister,
Swaying/ he killed his father,
They blow themselves up with pettiness
as if they were swaying with drink.

For such gentlemen   what
is the sunset or the sunrise?
They swallow emptiness,
these readers of newspapers.

For news   read: calumnies,
For news   read: embezzling,
in every column   slander
every paragraph some   disgusting thing.

46

With what, at the Last Judgement
will you come before the light?
Grabbers of small moments,
readers of newspapers.

Gone! lost! vanished! so,
the old maternal terror.
But mother, the Gutenberg Press
is more terrible than Schwarz' powder.

It's better to go to a graveyard
than into the   prurient
sickbay of scab-scratchers,
these readers of newspapers.

And who is it rots our sons
now in the prime of their life?
Those corrupters of blood
the *writers* of newspapers.

Look, friends   much
stronger than in these lines, do
I think this, when with
a manuscript in my hand

I stand before the face
there is no   emptier place
than before the absent
face of an editor of news
                    papers' evil filth.

1935

When I look at the flight of the leaves in
    their floating down on to the paving of cobbles
and see them swept up as if by an
    artist who has finished his picture at last

I think how (already nobody likes either
    the way I stand, or my thoughtful face)
a manifestly yellow, decidedly
    rusty leaf—has been left behind on the tree.

1936

From Poems to Chekhia

6

They took   quickly, they took   hugely,
   took the mountains and their entrails.
They took our coal, and took our steel
   from us, lead they took also and crystal.

They took the sugar, and they took the clover
   they took the North and took the West.
They took the hive, and took the haystack
   they took the South from us, and took the East.

Vary   they took and Tatras   they took,
   they took the near at hand and far away.
But   worse than taking paradise on earth from us
   they won the battle for our native land.

Bullets they took from us, they took our rifles
   minerals they took, and comrades too:
But while our mouths have spittle in them
   The whole country   is still armed.

1938

What tears in eyes now
weeping with anger and love
Czechoslovakia's tears
Spain in its own blood

and what a black mountain
has blocked the world   from the light.
It's time—It's time—It's time
to give back to God   his ticket.

I refuse to be. In
the madhouse   of the inhuman
I refuse   to live.
With the wolves of the market place

I refuse   to howl,
Among the sharks of the plain
I refuse to swim   down
where moving backs make a current.

I have no need of holes
for ears, nor prophetic eyes:
to your mad world there is
one answer: to refuse!

Epitaph

Just going out for a minute—
left your work (which the idle
call chaos) behind on the table.
And left the chair behind when   you went where?

I ask around all Paris, for it's
only in stories or pictures
that people rise to the skies:
where is your soul gone, where?

In the cupboard, two-doored like a shrine,
look   all your books are in place.
In each line the letters are there.
Where has it gone to, your face?

Your face
your warmth
your shoulder

where did they go?

Useless with eyes   like nails to
penetrate the black soil.
As true   as a nail in the mind
you are not here, not here.

It's useless   turning my eyes
and fumbling round the whole sky.
Rain. Pails of rain-water. But
you are not there, not there.

Neither one of the two. Bone is
too much bone. And spirit is too much spirit.
Where is the real you? All of you?
Too much here. Too much there.

And I won't exchange you for sand
and steam. You took me for kin,
and I won't give you up for a corpse
and a ghost: a here, and a there.

It's not you, not you, not you,
however much priests intone
that death and life are one:
God's too much God, worm—too much worm!

You are one thing, corpse and spirit.
We won't give you up for the smoke of
censers
or flowers
on graves

If you *are* anywhere, it's here in
us: and we honour best all those who
have gone by despising division.
It is all of you   that has gone.

3

Because once when you were young and bold
you did not leave me to rot alive among
bodies without souls or fall dead among walls
I will not let you   die altogether

Because, fresh and clean, you took me
out by the hand, to freedom   and brought spring leaves
in bundles into my house   I shall not
let you be grown over with weeds and forgotten.

And because you met the status of my
first grey hairs like a son   with pride
greeting their terror with a child's joy:
I shall not let you go grey into men's hearts.

The blow   muffled through years of
    forgetting, of not knowing:
That blow reaches me now like the song of a
    woman, or like horses neighing.

Through an inert building, a song of passion and
    the blow comes:
dulled by forgetfulness, by not knowing, which is
    a soundless thicket.

It is the sin of memory, which has no eyes or
    lips or flesh or nose,
the silt of all the days and nights
    we have been without each other

the blow is muffled with moss and waterweed:
    so ivy devours the
core of the living thing it is ruining
    —a knife through a feather bed.

Window wadding, our ears are plugged with it
    and with that other wool
outside windows of snow and the weight of spiritless
    years: and the blow is muffled.

The Poem of the Mountain

A shudder: off my shoulders
   with this mountain! My soul rises.
Now let me sing of sorrow which
   is my own mountain.

a blackness which I will
   never block out again:
Let me sing of sorrow
   from the top of the mountain!

A mountain, like the body of
a recruit mown down by shells,
wanting lips that were
unkissed, and a wedding ceremony

the mountain demanded those.
Instead, an ocean broke into its ears
with sudden shouts of hooray! Though
the mountain fought and struggled.

The mountain was like thunder!
A chest drummed on by Titans.
(Do you remember that last house
of the mountain—the end of the suburb?)

The mountain was many worlds!
And God took a high price for one.
Sorrow began with a mountain.
This mountain looked on the town.

Not Parnassus   not Sinai
simply a bare and military
hill. Form up! Fire!
Why is it then in my eyes
(Since it was October and not May)
that mountain was   Paradise?

3

On an open hand Paradise was offered,
(if it's too hot, don't even touch it!)
threw itself under our feet with all
its gullies and steep crags,

with paws of Titans, with all
its shrubbery and pines
the mountain siezed the skirts of our
coats, and commanded: stop.

How far from schoolbook Paradise
it was: so *windy*, when
the mountain pulled us down on our
backs. To itself. Saying: lie here!

The violence of that pull bewildered us.
How? Even now I don't know.
Mountain. Pimp. For holiness.
It pointed, to say: here.

4

How to forget Persephone's pomegranate
grain in the coldness of winter?
I remember lips half-opening to
mine, like the valves of a shell-creature

lost because of that grain, Persephone!
Continuous as the redness of lips,
and your eyelashes   were like jagged points
upon the golden angles of a star.

Not that passion is   deceitful or imaginary!
It doesn't lie. Simply, it doesn't last!
If only we could come into this world as though
we were common people in love

be sensible, see things as they are: this
is just a hill, just a bump in the ground.
(And yet they say it is by the pull of
abysses, that you measure height.)

In the heaps of gorse, coloured dim
among islands of tortured pines . . .
(In delirium/ above the level of
life)
    —Take me then. I'm yours.

Instead only the gentle mercies of
domesticity—chicks twittering—
because we came down into this world who
once lived at the height of heaven: in love.

The mountain was mourning, (and mountains do mourn,
their clay is bitter, in the hours of parting).
The mountain mourned: for the tenderness
(like doves) of our undiscovered mornings.

The mountain mourned: for our friendliness, for
that unbreakable kinship of the lips.
The mountain declared that everyone will
receive in proportion to his tears.

The mountain grieved because   life is a gypsy-camp,
and we go marketing all our life from heart to heart.
And this was Hagar's grief. To be
sent far away. Even with her child.

Also the mountain said that all things were a trick
of some demon, no sense to the game.
The mountain sorrowed. And we were silent.
leaving the mountain to judge the case.

The mountain mourned for what is now blood
and heat will turn only to sadness.
The mountain mourned. It will not let us go.
It will not let you lie with someone else!

The mountain mourned, for what is now
world and Rome will turn   only to smoke.
The mountain mourned, because we shall be with
others. (And I do not envy them!)

The mountain mourned: for the terrible load
of promises, too late for us to renounce.
The mountain mourned the ancient nature of
the Gordian knot of law and passion.

The mountain mourned for our mourning also.
For tomorrow! Not yet! Above our foreheads
will break—death's sea of—memories!
For tomorrow, when we shall realize!

That sound   what?   as if someone were
crying just nearby? Can that be it?
The mountain is mourning. Because we must go down
separately, over such mud,

into life which we all know is nothing but
mob market barracks:
That sound said: all poems of
mountains   are written *thus*.

8

Hump of Atlas, groaning
   Titan, this town where we
live, day in, day out, will come
   to take a pride in the mountain

where we defeated life—at cards, and
   insisted with passion *not to*
exist. Like a bear-pit.
   And the twelve apostles.

Pay homage to my dark cave,
   (I was a cave that the waves entered).
The last hand of the card game was
   played, you remember, at the edge of the suburb?

Mountain   many worlds   the
   gods take revenge on their own likeness!

And my grief began with this mountain
which sits above me now like my headstone.

Years will pass. And then   the inscribed
slab will be changed for tombstone and removed.
There will be summerhouses on our mountain.
Soon it will be hemmed in with gardens,

because in outskirts like this they say
the air is better, and it's easier to live:
so it will be cut into plots of land,
and many lines of scaffolding will cross it.

They will straighten my mountain passes.
All my ravines will be upended.
There must be people who want to bring happiness
into their *home*, to have *happiness*.

Happiness at home! Love without fiction.
Imagine: without any stretching of sinews.
I have to be a woman   and endure this!
(There was happiness—when you used to come,

happiness—in my home.) Love without any extra
sweetness given by parting. Or a knife.
Now on the ruins of our happiness
a town will grow: of husbands and wives.

And in that same blessed air, while
you can, everyone   should sin—
soon shopkeepers on holidays
will be chewing the cud of their profits,

thinking out new levels and corridors, as
everything leads them back   to their house!
For there has to be someone who needs
a roof with a stork's nest!

Yet under the weight of these foundations
the mountain will not forget   the game.
Though people go astray   they must remember.
And the mountain has   mountains of time.

Obstinate crevices and cracks remain;
in summer homes, they'll realize, too late,
this is no hill, overgrown with families, but
a volcano! Make money out of that!

Can vineyards ever hold the danger
of Vesuvius? A giant without fear cannot
be bound with flax. And the delirium
of lips alone has   the same power:

to make the vineyards stir and turn heavily,
to belch out their lava of hate.
Your daughters shall all become prostitutes
and all your sons turn into   poets!

You shall rear a bastard child my daughter!
Waste your flesh upon the gipsies, son!
May you never own a piece of fertile land
you   who take your substance from my blood.

Harder than any cornerstone, as
binding as the words of a dying man,
I curse you: do not look for happiness
upon my mountain   where you move like ants!

At some hour unforeseen, some time unknowable,
you will realize, the whole lot of you, how
enormous and without measure is
the mountain of God's seventh law.

Epilogue

There are blanks in memory   cataracts
on our eyes; the seven veils.
I no longer remember you separately
As a face but a white emptiness

without true features. All—is a
whiteness. (My spirit is one
uninterrupted wound.) The chalk of
details must   belong to tailors!

The dome of heaven was   built in a single frame
and oceans?   are featureless   a mass of
drops that cannot be distinguished. You
are unique. And love is no detective.

Let now some neighbour say whether your
hair is black or fair, for he can tell.
I leave that to physicians or watchmakers.
What passion has a use for such details?

You are a full, unbroken circle, a
whirlwind or   wholly turned to stone.
I cannot think of you apart from
love. There is an   equals sign.

(In heaps of sleepy down, and falls of
water, hills of foam, there is
a new sound, strange to my hearing,
instead of I   a regal *we*)

and though life's beggared now and
narrowed into—how things are—
still I cannot see you joined to
anyone: a
                    revenge of memory.

The Poem of the End

A single post, a point of rusting
   tin in the sky
marks the fated place we
   move to, he and I

on time   as death is
   prompt   strangely
too smooth the gesture of
   his hat to me

menace at the edges of his
   eyes   his mouth tight
shut   strangely too low is the
   bow he makes tonight

on time?   that false note in
   his voice, what
is it the brain alerts to and the
   heart drops at?

under that evil sky, that sign of
   tin and rust.
Six o'clock. There he is waiting
   by the post.

Now we kiss soundlessly, his
   lips stiff as
hands are given to queens, or
   dead people thus

round us the shoving elbows of
   ordinary bustle
and strangely irksome rises the
   screech of a whistle

howls like a dog screaming
    angrier, longer: what
a nightmare strangeness life is
    at death point

and that nightmare reached my waist
    only last night
and now reaches the stars, it has
    grown to its true height

crying silently love love until
    —Has it gone
six, shall we go to the cinema?
    I shout it! home!

And what have we come to?
 tents of nomads
thunder and drawn swords over
 our heads, some

terror we expect
 listen   houses
collapsing in the one
 word: home.

It is   the whine of a cossetted
 child lost, it is the
noise a baby makes for
 give and *mine*.

Brother in dissipation, cause
 of this cold fever, you
hurry now to get home just
 as men rush in leaving

like a horse jerking the
 line   rope down in the dust.
Is there even a building there?
 Ten steps before us.

A house on the hill   no higher   a
 house on the top of the hill and
a window under the roof   *is it*
 from the red sun alone

it is burning?   or is it my life
 which must begin again? how
simple poems are: it means I
 must go out into the night
                              (and talk to

who shall I tell my sorrow
    my horror greener than ice?
—You've been thinking too much.
    A solemn answer: yes.

And the embankment   I hold
   to water   thick and solid as
if we had come to the hanging
   gardens of Semiramis

to water   a strip as colourless
   as a slab for corpses
I am like a female singer holding
   to her music. To this wall.

Blindly   for you won't return
   or listen, even if I bend to
the quencher of all thirst, I am
   hanging at the gutter of a roof.

Lunatic. It is not the river
   (I was born naiad) that makes me
shiver now, she was a hand I held
   to, when you walked beside me, a lover

and faithful
            The dead are faithful
though not to all in their cells; if
   death lies on my left now,
it is at your side I feel it.

Now a shaft of astonishing light, and
   laughter   that cheap tambourine.
—You and I must   have a talk. And
   I shiver: let's be brave, shall we?

A blonde mist, a wave of
gauze ruffles, of human
breathing, smoky exhalations
endless talk   the smell of
what? of haste and filth
connivance   shabby acts   all
the secrets of business men
   and ballroom powder.

Family men   like bachelors
move in their rings like middle-aged boys
always joking   always laughing, and
calculating, always calculating
large deals   and little ones, they are
snout-deep in the feathers of some
business arrangement
   and ballroom powder.

(I am half-turned away   is this
our house? I am not mistress here)
Someone   over his cheque book
another bends to a kid glove hand
a third works at a delicate foot
in patent leather   furtively   the smell
rises of marriage-broking
   and ballroom powder.

In the window is the silver
bite of a tooth: it is the Star of Malta,
which is the sign of stroking of the love

that leads to pawing and to pinching.
(Yesterday's food perhaps   but
nobody worries if it smells slightly)
   of dirt, commercial tricks
      and ballroom powder.

The chain is too short perhaps even
if it is not steel but platinum?
Look how their three chins shake
like cows munching their own veal
above their sugared necks
the devils swing on a gas lamp
   smelling of business slumps
and another powder
made by Berthold Schwartz
                              genius
intercessor for people:
—You and I must   have a talk
—Let's be brave, shall we?

I catch a movement of his
   lips, but he won't
speak—You don't   love me?
   —Yes, but in torment

drained and driven to death
   (He looks round like an eagle)
—You call this   home? It's
   in the heart.—What *literature*!

For love is flesh, it is a
   flower flooded with blood.
Did you think it was just a
   little chat across a table

a snatched hour and back home again
   the way gentlemen and ladies
play at it? Either love is
   —A shrine?
               or else a scar.

A scar   every servant and guest
   can see (and I think silently:
love is a bow-string pulled
   back to the point of breaking).

Love is a bond. That has snapped for
   us   our mouths and lives part
(I begged you not to put a
   spell on me that holy hour

close on mountain heights of
   passion   memory is mist).
Yes, love is a matter of gifts
   thrown in the fire, for nothing.

The shell-fish crack of his mouth
    is pale, no chance of a smile:
—Love is a large   bed.
    —Or else an empty gulf.

Now his fingers begin to
    beat, no mountains
move. Love is—
                    —*Mine*: yes.
I understand. And so?

The drum beat of his fingers
    grows (scaffold and square)
—Let's go, he says. For me, let's
die, would be easier.

Enough cheap stuff   rhymes
    like railway hotel rooms, so:
—love means life   although
    the ancients had a different

name.
        —Well?
                    A scrap
of handkerchief in a fist
like a fish. Shall we go? How,
    bullet   rail   poison

death anyway, choose: I make no
    plans. A Roman, you
survey the men still alive
    like an eagle:
                    say goodbye.

75

6

I didn't want this, not
   this (but listen, quietly,
to want is what bodies do
   and now we are ghosts only).

And yet I   didn't say it
   though the time of the train is set
and the sorrowful honour of leaving
   is a cup given to women

or perhaps in madness I
   misheard you   polite liar:
is this the bouquet that you give your
   love, this blood-stained honour?

Is it? Sound follows
   sound clearly: was it goodbye
you said? (as sweetly casual
   as a handkerchief dropped without

thought) in this battle
   you are Caesar (What an
insolent thrust, to put the
   weapon of defeat, into my hand

like a trophy). It continues. To
   sound in my ears. As I bow.
—Do you always pretend
   to be forestalled in breaking?

Don't deny this, it
   is a vengeance of Lovelace
a gesture that does you credit
   while it lifts the flesh

from my bones. Laughter   the laugh of
    death. Moving. Without desire.
That is for others now
    we are shadows to one another.

Hammer the last nail in
    screw up the lead coffin.
—And now a last request.
    —Of course. Then say nothing

about us   to those who will
    come after me. (The sick
on their stretchers talk of spring.)
    —May I ask the same thing?

—Perhaps I should give you a ring?
    —No. Your look is no longer open.
The stamp left on your heart
    would be the ring on your hand.

So now   without any scenes
    I must swallow, silently, furtively.
—A book then? No, you give those
    to everyone, don't even write them

    books. . . .

So now   must   be no
so now   must   be no
must be no crying

In wandering tribes of
fishermen brothers
drink without crying

dance without crying
their blood is hot, they
pay without crying

pearls in a glass
melt, as they run their
world   without crying

Now I am going and this
Harlequin gives his
Pierrette a bone like
a piece of contempt

He throws her the honour
of ending the curtain, the last
word when one inch of lead in
the breast would be hotter and better

Cleaner. My   teeth
press my lips. I can
stop myself crying

pressing the sharpness
into the softest
so/ without crying

so tribes of nomads
die without crying
burn without crying.

So tribes of fishermen
in ash and song can
hide their dead man.

And the embankment. The last one.
  Finished. Separate, and hands apart
like neighbours avoiding one another. We
  walk away from the river, from my

cries. Falling salts of mercury
  I lick off without attention.
No great moon of Solomon
  has been set for my tears in the skies.

A post. Why not beat my forehead to
  blood on it? To smithereens! We are
like fellow criminals, fearing one
  another. (The murdered thing is love.)

Don't say these are lovers? Going into
  the night? Separately? To sleep with others?
You understand the future is up there?
  he says. And I throw back my head.

To sleep! Like newly-weds over their mat!
  To sleep! We can't fall into
step. And I plead miserably: take my
  arm, we aren't convicts to walk like this.

Shock! It's as though his *soul* has touched
  me   as his arm leans on mine. The electric
current beats along feverish wiring,
  and rips. He's leaned on my soul with his arm.

He holds me. Rainbows everywhere. What is more like a
    rainbow than tears? Rain, a curtain, denser
than beads. I don't know if such embankments can
    end. But here is a bridge and
                              —Well then?

Here? (The hearse is ready.)
    Peaceful   his eyes move
upward: couldn't you see me home?
    for the very last time.

Last   bridge   I won't
give up or take out my hand
this is the last bridge
the last bridging between

water   and firm land:
and I am saving these
coins for death
for Charon, the price of Lethe

this   shadow money
from my dark hand I press
soundlessly into
the shadowy darkness of his

shadow money it is
no gleam and tinkle in it
coins for shadows:
the dead have enough poppies

This bridge

Lovers for the most
part are without hope: passion
also is just
a bridge, a means of connection

It's warm: to nestle
close at your ribs, to move in
a visionary pause
towards nothing, beside nothing

no   arms no   legs
now, only the bone of my
side is alive where
it presses directly against you

life in that side
only, ear and echo is it: there
I stick like white to
egg yolk, or an eskimo to his fur

adhesive, pressing
joined to you: Siamese
twins are no nearer.
The woman you call mother

when she forgot
all things in motionless triumph
only to carry you:
she did not hold you closer.

Understand: we have
grown into one as we slept and
now I can't jump
because I can't let go your hand

and I won't be torn off
as I press close to you: this
bridge is no husband
but a lover: a just slipping past

our support: for the
river is fed with bodies!
I bite in like a tick
you must tear out my roots to be rid of me

like ivy   like a tick
inhuman   godless
to throw me away like a thing, when there is

no thing I ever prized
in this empty world of things.
Say this is only dream,
night still and afterwards morning

an express   to Rome?
Granada? I won't know myself
as I push off
the Himalayas of bedclothes.

But this dark is deep:
now I warm you with my blood, listen
to this flesh.
It is far truer than poems.

If you are warm, who
will you go to tomorrow for that?
This is delirium,
please say this bridge cannot

end
        as it ends.

9

Blatant as factory buildings,
    as alert to a call
here is the sacred and sublingual
    secret wives keep from husbands and

widows from friends, here is the full
    story that Eve took from the tree:
I am no more than an animal that
    someone has stabbed in the stomach.

Burning. As if the soul had been
    torn away with the skin. Vanished like steam
through a hole is that well-known foolish
    heresy called a soul.

That Christian leprosy:
    steam: save that with your poultices.
There never was such a thing.
    There was a body once, wanted to

live   no longer wants to live.

Forgive me! I didn't mean it!
  The shriek of torn entrails.
So prisoners sentenced to death wait
  for the 4 a.m. firing squad.

At chess perhaps with a grin
  they mock the corridor's eye.
Pawns in the game of chess:
  someone is playing with us.

Who? Kind gods or? Thieves?
  The peephole is filled with an
eye   and the red corridor
  clanks. Listen   the latch lifts.

One drag on tobacco, then
  spit, it's all over, spit,
along this paving of chess squares
  is a direct path   to the ditch

to blood. And the secret eye
  the dormer eye of the moon.

And now, squinting sideways, how
  far away you are already.

10

Closely, like one creature, we
start: there is our café!

There is our island, our shrine, where
in the morning, we people of the

rabble, a couple for a minute only,
conducted a morning service:

with things from country markets, sour
things seen through sleep or   spring.
The coffee was nasty there
entirely made from oats, (and

with oats you can extinguish
caprice in fine race-horses).
There was no smell of Araby
Arcadia was in

that coffee.

But how *she* smiled at us
and sat us down by her,
sad and worldly in her wisdom
a grey-haired paramour.

Her smile was solicitous
(saying: you'll wither! live!),
it was a smile at madness and being
penniless, at yawns   and love

and—this was the chief thing—
at laughter   without reason
smiles   with no deliberation
and our faces   without wrinkles.

Most of all   at youth
at passions   out of this climate
blown in from some other place
flowing from some other source

into that dim café
(burnous and Tunis) where
she smiled at hope and flesh
under old-fashioned clothes.

(My dear friend   I don't complain.
It's just another scar.)
To think how she saw us off,
that proprietress in her cap

stiff   as a Dutch hat. . . .

Not quite remembering, not quite
understanding, we are led away from the festival—
along our street!   no longer ours   that
we walked many times, and no more shall.

Tomorrow the sun will rise in the West.
—And then David will break with Jehovah.
—What are we doing?—We are *separating*.
—That's a word that means nothing to me.

It's the most inhumanly senseless
of words: *sep   arating*. (Am I one of a hundred?)
It is simply a word of four syllables and
behind their sound lies: emptiness.

Wait! Is it even correct in Serbian or
Croatian? Is it a Czech whim, this word.
Sep   aration! To *sep   arate!*
It is insane   unnatural

a sound to burst the eardrums, and spread out
far beyond the limits of longing itself.
Separation—the word is not in the Russian
language. Or the language of women. Or men.

Nor in the language of God. What are we—sheep?
To stare about us as we eat.
Separation—in what language is it,
when the meaning itself doesn't exist?

or even the sound! Well,—an empty one, like
the noise of a saw in your sleep perhaps.
Separation. That belongs to the school of
Khlebnikov's   nightingale-groaning

swan-like . . .
                    so how does it happen?
Like a lake of water running dry.
Into air. I can feel our hands touching.
To separate. Is a shock of thunder

upon my head—oceans rushing into
a wooden house. This is Oceania's
furthest promontory. And the streets are steep.
To separate. That means to go downward

downhill   the sighing sound of two
heavy soles   and at last a hand receives
the nail in it. A logic that turns
everything over. *To separate*

means we have to become
single creatures   again

we who had grown into one.

Dense as a horse mane is:
 rain in our eyes. And hills.
We have passed the suburb.
 Now we are out of town,

which is there   but not for us.
 Stepmother   not mother.
Nowhere   is lying ahead.
 And here   is where we fall.

A field with. A fence and.
 Brother and sister. Standing.
Life is   only a suburb:
 so you must build elsewhere.

Ugh, what a lost cause
 it is, ladies and gentlemen,
for the whole world is   suburb:
 Where   are the real towns?

Rain rips at us madly.
 We stand and break with each other.
In three months, these must be
 the first moments of sharing.

Is it true, God, that you even
 tried to borrow from Job?
Well, it didn't come off.
 Still. We are. Outside town.

Beyond it! Understand? Outside!
    That means   we've passed the walls.
Life is a place where it's forbidden
    to live. Like the Hebrew quarter.

And isn't it more worthy to
    become an eternal Jew?
Anyone not   a reptile
    suffers the same pogrom.

Life is for converts only
    Judases of all faiths.
Let's go to leprous islands
    or hell   anywhere   only not

life   which puts up with traitors, with
    those who are sheep   to butchers!
This paper which gives me the
    right to live—I stamp. With my feet.

Stamp! for the shield of David.
    Vengeance! for heaps of bodies
and they say after all (delicious) the
    Jews didn't want to live!

Ghetto of the chosen. Beyond this
    ditch. No mercy!
In this   most Christian of worlds
    all poets   are Jews.

This is how they sharpen knives on a
    stone, and sweep sawdust up with
brooms. Under my hands there is
    something wet and furry.

Now where are those twin male
    virtues: strength, dryness?
Here beneath my hand I can
    feel   tears. Not rain!

What temptations can still be
    spoken of? Property is   water.
Since I felt your diamond eyes under
    my hands, flowing.

There is no more I can lose. We have
    reached the end of ending.
And so I simply stroke, and
    stroke. And stroke your face.

This is the kind of pride we have:
    Marinkas   are Polish girls.
Since now the eyes of an eagle weep
    underneath these hands . . .

Can you be crying? My friend, my
    —everything! Please forgive me!
How large and salty now is the
    taste of that in my fist.

Male tears are—cruel! They
    rise over my head! Weep,
there will soon be others to
    heal any guilt towards me.

Fish of   identic-
   al sea. A sweep upward! like
. . . any dead shells and any
   lips upon lips.

In tears.
Wormwood
to taste.
—And tomorrow
when
I am awake?

A slope like a path   for
sheep. With town noises.
Three trollops approaching.
They are laughing. At tears.

They are laughing   the full noon of
their bellies shake, like waves!
They laugh at the
                              inappropriate
disgraceful, male

tears of yours, visible
through the rain   like scars!
Like a shameful   pearl on
the bronze of a warrior.

These first and last tears
pour them now—for me—
for your tears   are pearls
that I wear in my crown.

And my eyes are not lowered.
I stare through   the shower.
Yes, dolls of Venus
stare at me! because

This is a closer bond
than the transport of lying down.
The Song of Songs itself
gives place to our speech,

infamous birds as we are
Solomon bows to us, for
our simultaneous cries
are   something more than a dream!

And into the hollow waves of
darkness—hunched and level—
without trace—in silence—
something sinks like a ship.

Notes

No poet's voice can be exactly recorded in the medium of another language. Marina Tsvetayeva's is particularly difficult to capture, both because her consistent adherence to rhyme and to metrical regularity would, if copied in the English poems, probably enfeeble them, and because so many of the linguistic devices which she powerfully exploits (such as ellipsis, changes of word-order, the throwing into relief of inflectional endings) are simply not available in English. On the whole, the English versions are consciously less emphatic, less loudly-spoken, less violent, often less jolting and disturbing than the Russian originals. Most noticeable of all in Tsvetayeva's poems, expecially the later ones, are the very strong rhythm and the unprecedentedly vigorous syntax. There is, too, a somewhat idiosyncratic and highly emotional use of punctuation, particularly of exclamation marks and dashes.

Except in the case of 'The Poem of the Mountain', a literal version of which was prepared by Valentina Coe, and a number of earlier poems, where the literal version was dictated on to a tape-recorder, Elaine Feinstein and I worked as follows: I would write out each poem in English, keeping as close as made sense to the word-order of the Russian; joining by hyphens those English words which represented a single Russian word; indicating by oblique lines words whose order had to be reversed to be readable, and by asterisks phrases where several changes had had to take place; adding notes on metre, sound properties, play with word-roots, and specifically Russian connotations. All this *material* was then changed into poetry by Elaine Feinstein, who took those liberties with it that the new English poem demanded, but returned constantly to the Russian text to check the look, sound, and position of Tsvetayeva's own words.

To give one example—the opening of lyric 6 of 'The Poem of the End'. One of the most original and effective features of the poems making up this cycle is the way they tend to be structurally based each upon a single syntactic unit which is several times repeated almost identically. This determines the structure of every stanza in which it appears, throwing into different kinds of relief the words and phrases that are not part of it, and bringing a peculiar rhythm into the expressed emotion. When it ceases to recur, we read the rest of the poem in strong recollection of its shape.

In lyric 6 the dominant phrase (*italicized*, by me, in the extract below) is one that has the verb 'to hand' as its final and basic element, and involves the prominent use of the dative case. Each time, the phrase is in brackets and, each time, its last word comes as an enjambment. It occurs in stanzas 2, 3, and 5; is implied in stanza 4; and is referred to (through similar enjambment and rhythm) in stanza 6, where a sharp irony arises from the combination of the rhythm and pattern of that unit with the idea of 'dividing'—the opposite, one would think, of 'handing'. Here are these six stanzas, in Russian and 'literal' English. (I omit my notes.)

2

. . . .

(Da, v chas, kogda poyezd podan,   (Yes, at the-hour when the-train is-served,

Vy zhenshchinam, kak bokal,   *You to-women, like a-goblet,*

Pechal'nuyu chest' ukhoda   *The-sorrowful honour of-departure*

3

Vruchayete . . .)—Mozhet, bred?   *Hand . . .)*—Perhaps, delirium?

Oslyshalsa? (Lzhets uchtiviy,   I-misheard? (Courteous liar,

Lyubovnitse kak buket   *To-your-lover like a-bouquet*

Krovavuyu chest' razryva   *The-bloody honour of-rift*

4

Vruchayushchi . . .)—Vnyatno: slog   *Handing . . .)* (It's)-clear: syllable

Za slogom, itak—prostimsa,   After syllable, so—let's-say-goodbye,

Skazali vy? (Kak platok   You/said? (*Like a-handkerchief*

V chas sladostnovo beschinstva   *At the-hour of-voluptuous recklessness*

5

Uronenny . . .)—Bitvy sei   *Dropped . . .)*—Of-this/battle

Vy—Tsezar'. (O, vypad nagly!   You-are Caesar. (O, insolent/thrust!

Protivniku—kak trofei,   *To-(your)-opponent—like a-trophy,*

Im otdannuyu zhe shpagu   *The very sabre that he surrendered**

6

Vruchat'!)—Prodolzhayet. (Zvon   *To-hand!)*—It-continues. (Sound

V ushakh . . .)—Preklonyayus' dvazhdy: In (my)-ears . .) I-bow twice:

Vpervye operezhon   For-the-first-time I-am-forestalled

V razryve.—Vy eto kazhdoi?   In a-rift.—Do-you-(say) this to-every-(woman)?

7

Ne oprovergaite! Mest'	Don't deny-(it)! A-vengeance
Dostoinaya Lovelasa.	Worthy of-Lovelace.
Zhest, delayushchi vam chest',	*A-gesture doing you honour,*
A mne razvodyashchi myaso	*But for-me dividing the-flesh*

8

Ot kosti.   *From the-bone.*

All subsequent instances of the dative case in this poem stand out
strongly because of this established pattern: as, for example, the 'Do
you say this to everyone?' in stanza 6; the later plea not to speak of
their love to anyone coming after; and, especially, the final inter-
change about whether to give each other a parting gift such as a ring
or a book.

Different syntactic patterns dominate other lyrics in the cycle.
Their presence, as a fundamental structure, is typical of the whole
of 'The Poem of the End', and is a device which Tsvetayeva has
elaborated with complete originality.

*

page

4 'We are keeping an eye on the girls'
  kvass: a common Russian drink, non-alcoholic, made from
  fermented rye bread.
  Stenka Razin: a Cossack leader of the seventeenth-century peasant
  rebellion in Russia. According to legend, he sacrificed a Persian
  girl whom he loved to the river Volga.

5 'No one has taken anything away'
  This poem is addressed to the poet Osip Mandelstam (1892–
  1938) with whom Tsvetayeva had a close friendship. Derzhavin
  (1743–1816) was the most important Russian poet writing before
  Pushkin. Tsvetayeva gives his name to Mandelstam presumably
  because of the measured and classical nature of much of his
  poetry.

6 'You throw back your head'
  Again addressed to Mandelstam, who lived in St. Petersburg.
  Tsvetayeva shows—'gives'—him *her* native city, Moscow.

7 'Where does this tenderness come from?'
  Again addressed to Mandelstam.

9 'Today or tomorrow the snow will melt.'
  Rogozhin: a character in Dostoyevsky's novel *The Idiot* who sets
  out, with a knife, to kill the gentle hero of the novel, Prince
  Myshkin.

10 'Verses about Moscow'

Tsvetayeva addresses her small daughter.

'forty times forty churches': a phrase often used of Moscow.

Vagankovo: a well-known cemetery in Moscow.

11 Again addressed to Mandelstam to whom she is 'giving' her city.

Spassky gate, five cathedrals: these are in the Kremlin.

Inadvertent Joy: the name of a wonder-working icon of the Virgin Mary, and of the chapel containing it, not far from the Kremlin.

12 Peter the Great (1689–1725) founded St. Petersburg, which became his capital, replacing Moscow.

14 Panteleimon: a saint revered in the Orthodox Church, supposed to protect people's health.

The '*Iverskaya ikona*' is a wonder-working icon of the Virgin Mary, for which a special chapel was built and which was taken to the city of Vladimir in 1812.

15 *From* 'Insomnia'

Tsvetayeva perhaps speaks of her second child, who died.

23 'Poems for Akhmatova'

Anna Akhmatova: a poetess (1889–1966) contemporary of Tsvetayeva, who wrote many poems of love, sadness, and resignation. The exclamation in line 6 is, in Russian, '*akh*'—the first syllable of the poetess's name, as well as an expression of surprise, wonder, or sorrow.

'my melodious town', as 'my Kremlin' in the next poem: Tsvetayeva once again speaks as a poet of Moscow to one associated with St. Petersburg.

24 Tsarskoselsky: Akhmatova spent much of her youth in, and thereafter frequently visited, the imperial towns of Pavlovsk and Tsarskoye Selo, very near St. Petersburg. (Many Russian writers have lived at different times in Tsarskoye Selo; Pushkin attended the lycée there.)

25 'Poems for Blok'

Alexander Blok: the greatest Russian poet of this century (1880–1921), known as a Symbolist, with whom Tsvetayeva was never personally acquainted, although she met him briefly on two occasions.

Poems 1–8 in this series were written in 1916; no. 9 was written in 1920; and the rest, from no. 10, were written in August 1921, immediately after Blok's death.

'five signs': in the old orthography (altered after the Revolution, but always appealing to Tsvetayeva) Blok's name was spelt with five letters—these four plus a 'hard sign'.

28 Several images in this poem deliberately recall images and words

from poems by Blok himself: for example, spectre, knight, snow, wind.

30 The first two lines of this poem are a re-phrasing of the words of a well-known prayer sung in the Orthodox church ('Having come to the west of the sun, having seen the evening light'), and the words 'light of quiet, holy glory' in the last line but one recall the opening of that prayer ('Quiet light of holy glory').

31 Blok's native city was St. Petersburg, and Tsvetayeva once again contrasts 'her' Moscow, and its River Moscow, with 'his' St. Petersburg and its River Neva. The first phrase of the poem '*U menya v Moskve*' could also be translated 'In my Moscow'.

33 'red calico of Kaluga', literally 'Kaluga native calico': Tsvetayeva refers to the familar red calico made in Kaluga (where she spent the summers in her childhood), immediately suggestive of a typical peasant scene.

'talk about Germans': the poem was written in 1916.

34 This poem is dated 9 May 1920. On Tsvetayeva's manuscript is a note by her: 'On the day when the powder cellars were blown up in the Khodynka and the window panes were shattered in the Polytechnic Museum, where Blok was reading.' The Polytechnic Museum in Moscow was, in the years after the Revolution, often used for poetry readings to large audiences. In her essay 'Downpour of Light' (about Pasternak) Tsvetayeva again refers to Blok's reading at the Polytechnic Museum.

'blue cloak' is an image from Blok's poem '*O podvigakh, o doblestyakh, o slave*', written in 1908 and addressed to his wife. The relevant lines are (in the version by Jon Stallworthy and Peter France) 'You wrapped yourself round in a blue cloak sadly/and went into the wet night on your own'.

'the days that wait for us . . . : this refers to Blok's poem of 1910, '*Golos iz khora*', with its lines: 'You will call for the sun's rising—/the sun will lie low.'

44 'Homesickness!'

Kamchatka is in Siberia.

49 *From* 'Poems to Chekhia'

'Vary': Karlovy vary, or Karlsbad, a famous spa in western Czechoslovakia. By mentioning it along with 'Tatry', the Tatras, mountain ranges in the eastern part of that country, Tsvetayeva means to say that the Germans took the *whole* of the country, from West to East, and all the pleasures that it offered.

'spittle': the poem is headed by a sentence from the newspapers of March 1939: 'The Czechs went up to the Germans and spat.'

'they won': 'won' in Russian can also mean 'took'.

50 'give back to God his ticket': this seems to be a reference to Ivan

Karamazov (in Dostoyevsky's *Brothers Karamazov*), who defiantly offered back to God his entrance ticket to Heaven so long as that Heaven is built upon, or despite, the suffering of children on earth.

51 'Epitaph'

The series of poems called 'Epitaph' are about the little-known poet N. P. Gronsky (1909–1934) with whom Tsvetayeva made friends in Paris in 1928. He was killed in a street accident.

The last line is built upon a pun: '*Sovsem ushol. So svem ushol—*' 'Completely gone. With everything gone.' The Russian for 'completely' or 'forever' is a compound word made up of 'with' and 'everything'.

55 'The Poem of the Mountain'

This and 'The Poem of the End' are about the end of a love affair which Tsevtayeva had while living in Prague (1922–1925).

61 Hagar: the slave and concubine of the patriarch Abraham, who bore him a son, Ishmael; was sent away with the child at the insistence of Abraham's wife; and went to live in the Arabian desert.

63 'twelve apostles': Tsvetayeva is probably referring to the clock tower on the Old Town Square in Prague where, each hour, the figures of the twelve apostles appear and disappear above the dial.

67 'The Poem of the End'

The fourteen poems of this cycle, some divided into two or three lyrics, are about the poet's meeting with her lover and their walk through Prague, or a part of that walk, during which they agree to end their relationship. Feelings, sensations, thoughts about feelings and sensations and about their situation, dominate the poem. External things come in fragmentarily and unobtrusively. As the poem becomes clear and effective only when one does notice what externally 'happens', a brief summary of the narrative element may be useful:

1. She meets him 'at the appointed place'. His behaviour is ominously polite.
2. She thinks of 'house' and 'home'.
3. They walk by the embankment of the river and, coming to a café, decide to go in and 'have a talk'.
4. They sit in the café, in an atmosphere of prostitution and commercial vulgarity.
5. They talk across the café table. He is nervous and she is going to cry. They decide to part.
6. They talk on. She finds herself starting to cry, and tries not to.
7. They go out and continue walking by the embankment.

8. They cross the bridge.
9. She cries; thinks about 'prison'.
10. They pass another café—which they used to frequent when they were in love. She thinks about 'separation'.
11–12. They walk further out of the city. She thinks about the concepts 'suburb' and 'out of town'. They go up a hill (which seems to be the 'mountain' of the preceding cycle) and look down over the city with its Jewish Quarter.
13. He weeps and she comforts him.
14. They come down hill again into the city. Prostitutes laugh at them. They part.

69 'a window under the roof   *is it*
   from the red sun alone

   it is burning?

   This is a rephrasing of lines in a poem by Blok the last stanza of which runs (translated literally):

   > What is tenderer than the moon, what is higher than sunset twilights?
   > Know for yourself, be silent, don't say it to your friends:
   > On the top floor, there, under the high roof,
   > A window, burning not from the red sun alone . . .

70 'who shall I tell my sorrow': words from the Psalter.
71 Semiramis: an Assyrian princess (*c.* 800 B.C.) famous for her hanging gardens, one of the Seven Wonders of the World.
72 Star of Malta: the emblem of a medieval knightly order.
73 powder of Berthold Schwartz: gunpowder.
76 Lovelace: the seducer hero of Richardson's novel, *Clarissa*.
77 'the stamp left on your heart/would be the ring on my hand': Tsvetayeva alludes to the Song of Songs (8.6): 'Set me as a seal upon thine heart, as a seal upon thine arm, for love is strong as death, jealousy as cruel as the grave.'
87 burnous: an Arab cloak.
88 Khlebnikov: a Russian Futurist poet.
92 Marinka: diminutive of Marina, a common Polish name (and well known to Russians from the princess in Pushkin's *Boris Godunov*).

A. Livingstone

Index of Titles and First Lines